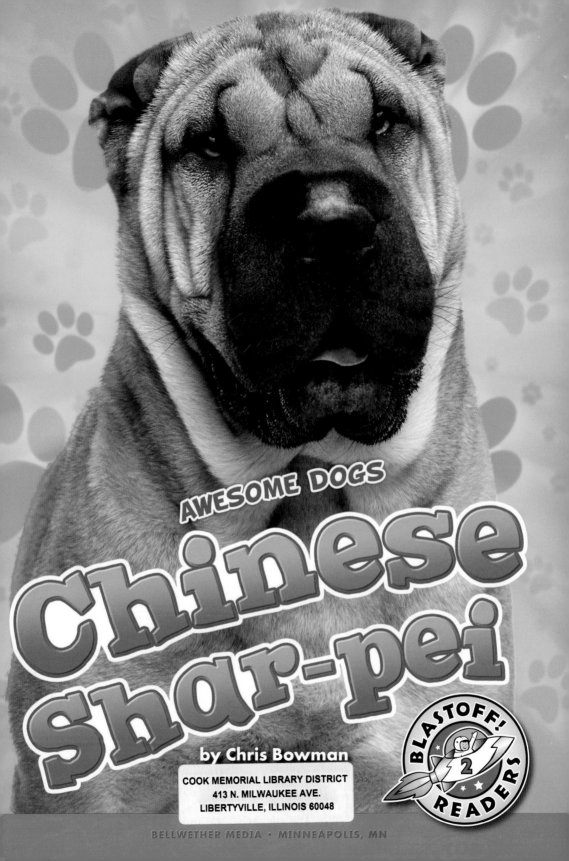

AWESOME DOGS

Chinese Shar-pei

by Chris Bowman

BLASTOFF! 2 READERS

BELLWETHER MEDIA · MINNEAPOLIS, MN

Note to Librarians, Teachers, and Parents:

Blastoff! Readers are carefully developed by literacy experts and combine standards-based content with developmentally appropriate text.

Level 1 provides the most support through repetition of high-frequency words, light text, predictable sentence patterns, and strong visual support.

Level 2 offers early readers a bit more challenge through varied simple sentences, increased text load, and less repetition of high-frequency words.

Level 3 advances early-fluent readers toward fluency through increased text and concept load, less reliance on visuals, longer sentences, and more literary language.

Level 4 builds reading stamina by providing more text per page, increased use of punctuation, greater variation in sentence patterns, and increasingly challenging vocabulary.

Level 5 encourages children to move from "learning to read" to "reading to learn" by providing even more text, varied writing styles, and less familiar topics.

Whichever book is right for your reader, Blastoff! Readers are the perfect books to build confidence and encourage a love of reading that will last a lifetime!

This edition first published in 2020 by Bellwether Media, Inc.

No part of this publication may be reproduced in whole or in part without written permission of the publisher. For information regarding permission, write to Bellwether Media, Inc., Attention: Permissions Department, 6012 Blue Circle Drive, Minnetonka, MN 55343.

Library of Congress Cataloging-in-Publication Data

Names: Bowman, Chris, 1990- author.
Title: Chinese Shar-Pei / by Chris Bowman.
Description: Minneapolis, MN : Bellwether Media, Inc., [2020] | Series: Blastoff! Readers: Awesome Dogs | Audience: Age 5-8. | Audience: K to Grade 3. | Includes bibliographical references and index.
Identifiers: LCCN 2018057361 (print) | LCCN 2018058645 (ebook) | ISBN 9781618915474 (ebook) | ISBN 9781644870068 (hardcover : alk. paper)
Subjects: LCSH: Chinese Shar-Pei–Juvenile literature.
Classification: LCC SF429.C48 (ebook) | LCC SF429.C48 B69 2020 (print) | DDC 636.72–dc23
LC record available at https://lccn.loc.gov/2018057361

Editor: Al Albertson   Designer: Laura Sowers

Printed in the United States of America, North Mankato, MN.

Table of
Contents

Chinese shar-pei are calm and **loyal** dogs. Their name can be shortened to shar-pei.

This word means "sand skin" in Chinese. These dogs have rough **coats**!

Chinese shar-pei have an uncommon look. They have wide, flat faces with short ears.

Small eyes peek from the folds of their skin. Their tongues are often bluish black.

Shar-pei are known for their **wrinkles**. This loose skin is thought to keep them safe from **attacks**.

wrinkles

Their wrinkles fade with age.

blue

Shar-pei have short, thick fur that comes in many colors.

Chinese Shar-pei Coats

red   fawn   cream

Some coats are blue or red.
Others are **fawn** or cream!

History of Chinese Shar-pei

Shar-pei were first **bred** in China over 2,000 years ago.

China

N W E S

The loyal dogs **protected** their families and herded animals on farms. They were also great hunters.

Chinese Shar-pei Profile

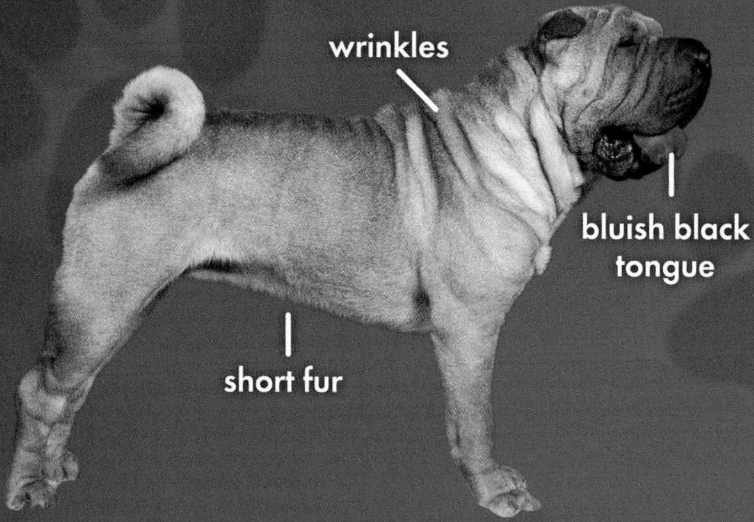

wrinkles

bluish black
tongue

short fur

Life Span: 8 to 12 years

Trainability:

(1) (2) (3) (4) (5) (6)

Hardest to train   Easiest to train

By 1950, few people in
China owned dogs.

Shar-pei almost disappeared.
But some were saved!

Soon, Chinese shar-pei became popular in the United States. The **American Kennel Club** added them in 1992.

Today, the **breed** is in the **Non-sporting Group**.

Wrinkled Watchdogs

Chinese shar-pei can be **territorial**. They keep watch for their families.

Many enjoy working
as guard dogs.

Shar-pei like to be inside
the house. They are happiest
with adults and older children.

They want to keep
everyone safe!

Glossary

American Kennel Club—an organization that keeps track of dog breeds in the United States

attacks—acts that cause harm

bred—purposely mated two dogs to make puppies with certain qualities

breed—a type of dog

coats—the hair or fur covering some animals

fawn—a light brown color

loyal—having constant support for someone

Non-sporting Group—a group of dog breeds that do not usually hunt or work

protected—to have kept something or someone safe

territorial—wanting to keep an area safe

wrinkles—lines in skin or fur

To Learn More

AT THE LIBRARY

Gagne, Tammy. *The Dog Encyclopedia for Kids.* North Mankato, Minn.: Capstone Young Readers, 2017.

Polinsky, Paige V. *Chinese Shar-Peis.* Minneapolis, Minn.: Abdo Publishing, 2017.

Schuetz, Kari. *Pugs.* Minneapolis, Minn.: Bellwether Media, 2017.

ON THE WEB

FACTSURFER

Factsurfer.com gives you a safe, fun way to find more information.

1. Go to www.factsurfer.com.

2. Enter "Chinese shar-pei" into the search box and click 🔍.

3. Select your book cover to see a list of related web sites.

Index

The images in this book are reproduced through the courtesy of: Eric Isslee, cover, pp. 5, 11 (middle), 11 (right), 12; Alexeysun, pp. 4-5; slyusareva oxana, p. 6; sanjagrujic, pp. 6-7; bruev, pp. 8-9; Yuliya Khovbosha, p. 9; LTD Photographic, pp. 10-11; Zoja Emeliananove, p. 11 (left); Martin Parker, pp. 12-13; TatyanaPanova, p. 14; Tierfotoagentur/ Alamy, pp. 14-15; Ansaharju, pp. 16-17; Grigorita Ko, p. 17; GROSSEMY VANESSA/ Alamy, pp. 18-19, 21; f8grapher, p. 19; kate_sept2004, 20-21.